LEARN HOW TO INCREASE YOUR CHANCES OF
WINNING THE LOTTERY

WRITTEN BY
RICHARD LUSTIG

I dedicate this book to my son, Nicholas, who encouraged me
(okay, he actually hounded me) to write this book.

I wish to thank the following people:

First, my wife, Cosetta, who for over twenty-five years has been
not only my partner in life, but my best friend as well.

My daughter, Jennifer, and her husband, Shaun, who believed in
my method, followed it, and also won a lottery game grand-prize.

My brother, Donald, who has been using my method through the writing of
this book. He has not won a grand prize yet, but maybe he soon will!

My mother-in-law, Lilia, who has been a believer from the very first grand prize I won.

And finally, my late mother, Sylvia, who through my whole life always believed in me.

TABLE OF CONTENTS

WITHDRAWN

TESTIMONIALS

Here is what people are saying about my method:

"My husband and I used lotto method, and within months of starting the method we hit a Mega Money jackpot for 2 million dollars! It was really easy to follow, you only play what you can and you can still win!
Shaun and I will only play lotto from now on using these strategies."

Jennifer and Shaun
Florida

"Since we've been using your method, we have definitely been winning more than we used to. It's easy to follow."

Yvette & Dale
Florida

"I just wanted to let you know that my husband and I read through your lottery method last night, and it's great. It seems to be just simple logic, and it makes sense."

Kate
Illinois

"Hi, thank you for e-mailing me your book on winning the lottery. Since you have been so successful I take what you say seriously and will try to follow it since you have a proven record. As far as scratch-offs, I will definately try your idea as it makes a lot of sense."

Marilyn
Alabama

INTRODUCTION

Welcome, and congratulations on purchasing my book.

Before we begin, I want to point out that you can go into any bookstore or any Web site on the Internet where other people offer some sort of lottery game winning method. However, if you do some research and check them out, you will find that most of the authors of those books or Web sites have never won a lottery game grand prize; if they have, maybe they have won one or two times. Since the writing of this book, I have won six (that's right, I said six) lottery game grand prizes.

Another Win!

That's right! Since putting this book into production, I have won my seventh grand prize, this one for $98,992.92. My system to win the lottery works. It's a good day!

August 9, 2010

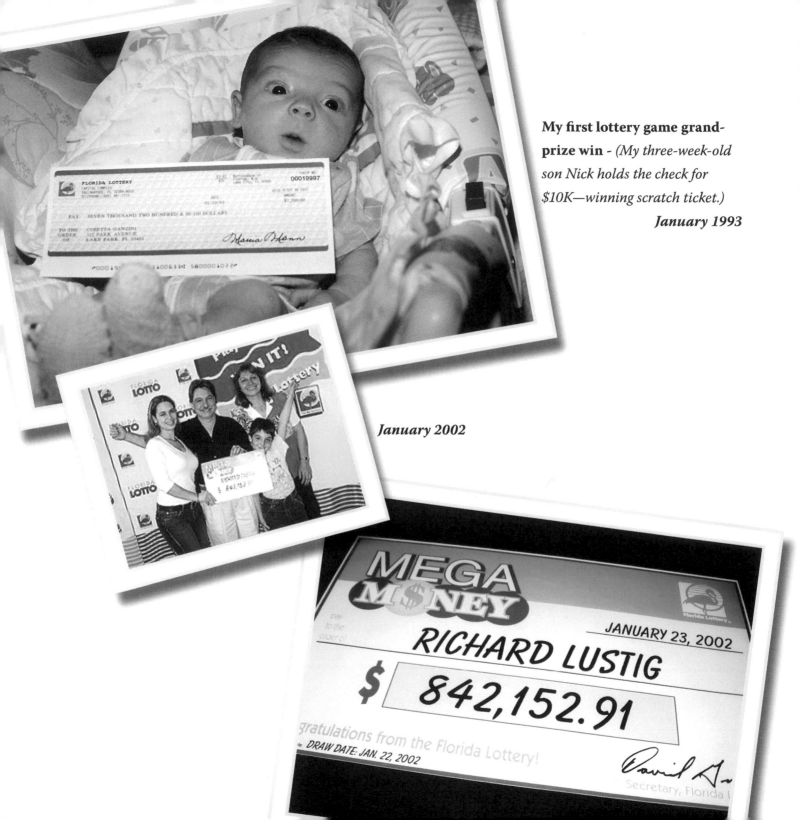

My first lottery game grand-prize win - *(My three-week-old son Nick holds the check for $10K—winning scratch ticket.)*

January 1993

January 2002

In addition to the grand prizes I've won, I have won several cash prizes that were too large to be paid out by the local store at which I buy my tickets. Therefore, I make several trips each year to the lottery district office to collect those winnings. The folks at the lottery office know me very well.

My name is Richard Lustig and I am about to share with you the playing methods I created to increase your chances of winning lottery games. First of all, let me start out by saying that even if you follow these methods I am about to share with you, **I make no guarantees or promises that you will win anything**—but I sincerely hope that you do!

All I can say is, these are the methods I and members of my family have followed, and we have won several large lottery game grand prizes. By the way, don't just take my word for it; check out www.floridalottery.com. You will see me and my daughter and son-in-law (Jennifer and Shaun Olson) on that Web site.

So let's begin!

The first and most important thing to remember is, **don't spend more than you can afford**. Some people go crazy and spend more money on playing lottery games than they should. Whether it is one dollar per week or one hundred dollars per week, the amount you choose to spend each week should be within your budget. Nothing is worth risking your family's financial security. I will say this, however: the more you play, the better your chances are of winning. But *be smart.*

CHAPTER ONE

SCRATCH TICKETS

Let's start out with scratch tickets. One of my grand-prize wins was a scratch ticket, and these are the hardest to win. The state will print a set amount of tickets for each scratch game. Within the printed tickets, there will be a fixed number of grand prizes.

These tickets are disbursed throughout the state, so there is no way of knowing if even one of the grand-prize winning tickets has even been sent to the city you live in. That doesn't mean it hasn't, and even if one of those grand-prize tickets makes it to your city, there is no guarantee that it will end up at the store at which you buy your tickets.

I will tell you that I have won not only a money grand prize on scratch tickets, but also two separate grand-prize trips.

I don't keep buying different tickets for different games. I hear people say to the clerk, "I'll take one of those and one of those and two of those."

This is like trying to shoot at a target with a blindfold on. I pick the scratch game that has the grand prize I want to win and only play that game. I usually go for the scratch ticket that offers the largest grand prize.

Also, state lotteries usually have a Website. This is where I check out which scratch games still have unclaimed grand prizes. Of course, I make sure I don't pick a game in which all the grand-prize tickets are gone. For example, let's say the game I choose is a $10 ticket. I start out by buying ten tickets ($100.00). I then use the money I win on those tickets to buy more tickets; I don't buy any additional tickets using additional money. I keep doing this as long as I keep winning any amount.

For example, if out of those tickets I win $60, then I buy six more tickets. Then if out of those tickets I win $20, I buy two more tickets, and so on. In this example, I just played $180 worth of tickets for only $100.

Now let's say one of those tickets is a winning $500 ticket. When the stores put out a new book of those tickets, there are thirty tickets in a book ($300 worth). I buy an unopened book and put the additional $200 in my pocket. With that $300 worth of tickets, I start over with the process I described above. If or when I find no winners in a batch of tickets, then I start all over again with $100.

The method is simple. Buying tickets from the same game over and over again gives me a chance of finding winning tickets in that game—hopefully one of the grand-prize tickets.

CHAPTER TWO

SECOND-CHANCE DRAWINGS

Some scratch-ticket games offer a second-chance drawing. In these games, you may mail in your losing tickets for a chance to win a second-chance drawing. Second-chance drawing prizes include cash, trips, cars, motorcycles, etc.

Two of my lottery grand-prize wins were in second-chance drawings.

Most people throw away their losing tickets. They either don't pay attention to the rules of the game they are playing and don't realize that there is a second-chance drawing associated with that particular game, or they just don't want to be bothered with having to address an envelope, put a stamp on it, and mail it. Therefore, those people who do enter have a very good chance of winning.

So in these games, I don't throw away my losing tickets; I mail them in. Obviously, the more I enter, the better my chances are at winning.

But one thing is for sure: you can't win if you don't enter.

FLORIDA LOTTERY

JEB BUSH
Governor

DAVID GRIFFIN
Secretary

October 17, 2001

Mr. Richard Lustig
P.O. BOX 770850
Orlando, FL 32877

Subject: Your Florida Lottery *"Elvis™* Graceland® Trip" Prize

Dear Mr. Lustig:

Congratulations on becoming a Grand Prize Winner in the Florida Lottery's ELVIS Scratch-off Game! You and your travel companion will experience Elvis Presley like never before on your trip to the home of *The King of Rock and Roll*. The Florida Lottery is working with Media Drop-in Productions (MDI) in arranging your trip to Graceland.

You should receive your Elvis Gift Packs within the next two to three weeks. You will receive your cash prize and your gift certificates approximately two weeks before your scheduled trip. Your admission tickets to Graceland attractions and Elvis Presley's Memphis® Restaurant dinner coupon will be provided to you upon check-in at the Heartbreak Hotel®.

What now?

To claim your prize, you need to complete the two forms enclosed with this letter. One form asks for information on whom you will be traveling with and how you prefer to travel. The other form asks for information on when you would like to schedule your trip. It's very important that you complete both forms, sign them and return them to MDI as soon as possible, so final arrangements can be made for your trip. A postage-paid envelope is enclosed for your convenience.

250 MARRIOTT DRIVE • CAPITOL COMPLEX • TALLAHASSEE, FL •
www.flalottery.com

My two second-chance drawing grand prizes were an all-expenses-paid trip to Los Angeles, California, to audition for *Wheel of Fortune* (August 2000) and an all-expenses-paid trip to Memphis, Tennessee, with a visit to *Elvis' Graceland* plus accommodations at *The Heartbreak Hotel* and numerous prizes along with the trip (October 2001).

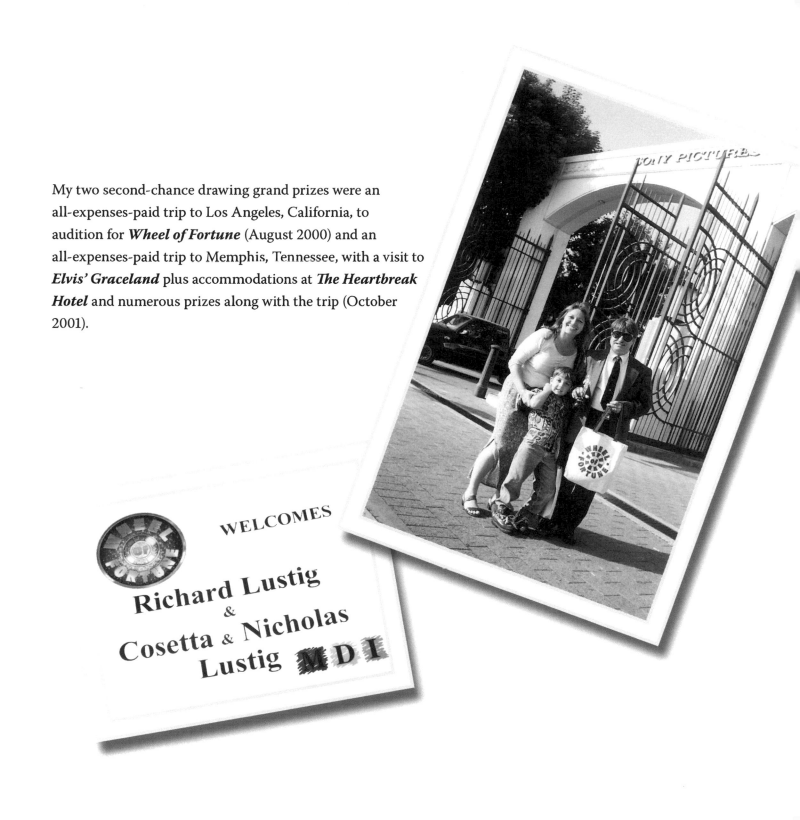

WELCOMES

Richard Lustig
&
Cosetta & Nicholas
Lustig M D I

CHAPTER THREE

LOTTERY NUMBER GAMES

Four of my lottery game grand-prize wins were from lottery number games. My method is simple math.

Let's say the odds of winning are 1 in 24,000,000. If I buy one ticket, then those are my odds. If I buy ten tickets, then my odds are 1 in 2,400,000. With one hundred tickets, my odds are 1 in 240,000, and so on. So obviously, the more tickets I buy in any one drawing, the better my odds of winning. **But remember what I said: don't buy more than you can afford.**

Now this is going to sound weird, but it's just simple math.

If you buy one ticket, your odds are 1 in 24,000,000. Let's say I lose and buy the same set of numbers for the next drawing, now my odds are 1 in 23,999,999. I know, *big deal,* right? But it's practically impossible for the same winning numbers to come up again, so every time I buy those same numbers, my odds get better and better. They go from 1 in 23,999,998 to 1 in 23,999,997, and so on. I know that sounds ridiculous, but this is simple, logical math. Ask any math professor, and he or she will tell you that what I am saying is true.

I never change my numbers. Let me repeat that. I never change my numbers!

Now, how do you pick your numbers?

Some people use family events, birthdays, anniversaries, etc. Some people use stock market numbers. Heck, some people take the numbers off a fortune cookie! You know what? It doesn't matter where you get your numbers from. Just remember. Never change your numbers. Let me repeat that. *Never change your numbers.*

Here is one thing you do want to do regarding the numbers you are going to play. You certainly don't want to play a set of numbers that has already been drawn at some point during the history of that particular numbers game that you are going to play. The odds of your numbers being drawn and you being a winner in any lottery numbers game are stacked high enough against you as it is. I don't know if there has ever been a set of numbers that has ever come up twice in any lottery numbers game. I can't imagine that happening; the odds have got to be astronomical.

As far as I know, all lotteries have a Web site. In Florida, you can go to the lottery Web site and find a field in which you can insert a set of numbers and search to see if that set of numbers has ever come up before.

So once you have decided what set, or sets, of numbers you are going to play, be sure to do that search. As I said before, you definitely don't want to be playing numbers that have come up before.

Next, I play those numbers for every draw.

I never miss a draw. I repeat: I never miss a draw.

If I miss a draw, I know what will probably happen. The night I don't play my numbers will be the night that my numbers will be drawn!

In Florida, the card you fill out to play the lottery has ten chances on it, with each chance costing $1. If you play all ten, your odds of winning become 1 in 2,400,000 (as in the example I gave earlier.).

I keep track of each card I fill out. I put the number 1 on the back of my first card, the number 2 on the back of the second, and so on.

So how many cards do I play? I base this decision on a couple of things.

First, our state lottery usually starts out with a $3-million jackpot. So I buy three cards ($30, thirty chances to win). If no one wins, the jackpot may go up to $6 million for the next drawing. I will then buy six cards ($60, sixty chances to win). So whatever the upcoming jackpot is, I play $10 in tickets for each million dollars.

Example: $15-million jackpot = fifteen cards ($150)

Remember, the backs of my cards are numbered, so card number 1 always gets played first. Then card number 2, and then card number 3, etc. Remember, once I fill out a card, whether it's the first card or the tenth card, I never change those numbers. I always play the same numbers on the same cards in the same order.

Second, just like in the scratch games, **I use my winnings to buy more tickets.**

So as an example, let's say the jackpot is at $3 million. I bought three cards ($30) and won $50, but someone won the jackpot. The next jackpot is again at $3 million, so I take the $50 I won and buy my first five cards ($50). I just played $80 in tickets, but I only paid $30. I win $250, I play twenty-five cards. Get the idea?

So the number of cards I play is determined by the jackpot and/or the amount of money I won in the last drawing.

The minimum amount I buy is based on the jackpot. The maximum amount I buy is based on the amount I just won.

CHAPTER FOUR

LOTTERY NUMBER GAMES—EXTRA BALL

Some lottery numbers games have you pick an extra ball. For example, in Florida there are two games that fall into this category—Mega Money, which is a Florida-only game, and Powerball, which is a multistate game of which Florida is a part.

For this example, we will talk about the Mega Money game (which, by the way, is one of the lottery games in which I won a lottery game grand prize). In this game, you pick four numbers from one to forty-four and one number from one to twenty-two (the final number is called the mega ball). When you buy your tickets, make sure each ticket has a different mega ball number on it. If you buy ten tickets and three of the mega ball numbers are repeated, then you only have seven out of twenty-two chances of winning. If you buy ten tickets and each ticket has a different mega ball number on it, then you now have ten out of twenty-two chances of winning. If you buy twenty-two tickets, you should have all twenty-two mega ball numbers covered, and this means you are guaranteed to win. In this particular lottery game, if you match only the mega ball number, you win a free ticket good for the next drawing.

If you match the mega ball number and one, two, three or all four of the other numbers, you win money. The amount of money you win depends on how many of the other numbers you match, but even if you only match the mega ball number and win a free ticket, it's better than not winning anything at all.

C H A P T E R   F I V E

LOTTERY EXTRA OR POWERPLAY

Some lottery games have what's called **"Extra"** or **"Powerplay."** This means that a separate number, usually between two and five, is chosen, and then all of the non-jackpot winning amounts are multiplied by that number.

For example, if the number that night is three and you had a ticket that would normally pay out $10, it would now pay out $30. Sounds great, right? Wrong! Here's the catch.

In order for you to be eligible to have your $10 ticket now be worth $30, you must pay an additional $1. This means that the ticket will cost you $2. Let's say you buy thirty tickets, which normally would cost you $30. If you had a $10 winner, you would lose $20, but if you paid the extra $1 per ticket, you would have paid $60 for those thirty tickets, which means you would lose $50.

The biggest problem with this situation is that paying the extra money does not increase your chances of winning. As we all know, a person loses more times than he or she wins. So according to the above example, the normal cost for thirty tickets is $30. If none of the tickets is a winner, you lose $30. If you pay the extra $1 per ticket, the cost for thirty tickets is $60. If none of the tickets is a winner, you lose $60. As you can see, the extra charge for the Extra or Power Play only works in your favor…

If you win.

If you win a large enough amount.

If the extra number multiplies your cost to come out ahead.

That's a lot of 'ifs'.

CHAPTER SIX

ONE-TIME LOTTERY GAMES

The lottery usually offers special games twice a year. For instance, in Florida there is the July 4 Firecracker Millionaire Raffle. In these types of games, there are only so many tickets available to buy. Once all the tickets are sold, no one else can buy a ticket for that drawing.

If you listen to all the advertising for these types of games, the pitch is that because a limited number of tickets are sold, the odds of winning are better than those of the normal lottery games. This may be true, but the only way to have a better chance of winning over everybody else is to buy a lot of tickets. The tickets for these games are usually $20 each.

So what is a lot of tickets? That amount is different to each person.

One person might not think twice about buying one hundred tickets that would cost them $2,000. But most people can afford only one or two tickets. To these people, the chances of winning are very slim, and at $20 a ticket—well, you get the idea.

Part of the success of my method (in the numbers games) is the playing of the same numbers over and over again. By doing this, each time you lose, your chances in the next drawing become better than your chances of winning the previous drawing. With these one-time games, you don't get that advantage.

CHAPTER SEVEN

WHEN TO BUY YOUR TICKETS

One of the worst things I see people do is wait until the last minute to buy tickets for a lottery game drawing. As an example, the Florida lotto game draw occurs twice a week, on Wednesdays and Saturdays. People will wait until they leave work on the day of the drawing to go buy their tickets for that night's game.

Why?

They get to the store, and what do they find? A long line of other people who are doing the same thing. Why put yourself through that ordeal?

I value my time more than that, so I always buy my tickets for the next drawing on the day after the most recent drawing.

For example, if a drawing is held Wednesday night and the next drawing will be held Saturday night, I buy my tickets for Saturday night's drawing on Thursday morning. No lines, no wasted time, no problem.

CHAPTER EIGHT

DO I HAVE A WINNING TICKET?

Okay, so you bought your tickets, they held the drawing, and now you want to know if you won.

Here is another thing I see people do that is such a time waster and is unfair to people who are waiting in line to buy tickets. I'm in line to buy my tickets, just like everybody else, and the person in front of me steps up to the counter, hands the clerk a bunch of tickets, and says, "Could you check these tickets and tell me if I am a winner?"

First of all, the clerks are not supposed to do that, and second of all, guess what? Nine out of ten times, the bunch of tickets that person just gave to the clerk doesn't contain any winners. That person just wasted the clerk's time, that person's own time, my time, and the time of everyone who is waiting in line.

There are several ways to find out if any of your tickets are winners.

First, There is usually a local television station that broadcasts the drawings live. You can stay up on the night of the drawing and watch it on TV.

Second, most newspapers have a section in which they list the winning numbers.

Third, there is usually a lottery phone number on your tickets that you can call to get the latest lottery results.

Fourth, lotteries have Internet Web sites where you can check the numbers on your tickets to see if you are a winner.

And finally, there are two ways to check for the winning numbers at the store where you bought your tickets. The store will have the latest lottery numbers drawn printed out on a stack of tickets, which will be sitting on the counter for anyone who wants them. And, usually right next to the lottery machine where you buy your tickets, there is a scanner. You can insert your ticket and it will tell you if it is a winner.

The other day I was in line and a man was standing there with some tickets in his hand, obviously waiting to have the clerk check them for him. I pointed out the scanner to the man and told him he could check his tickets on his own and therefore didn't have to wait for his turn in line. He said, "I don't trust that machine." Folks, it's part of the same system as the machine that the clerk uses.

So you see, there are many ways to check your tickets to see if you are a winner.

Very important—If you have a winning ticket of at least $1,000, turn the ticket over before you do anything else.

On the back, there is a place to fill in your name, address, etc. Be sure you do this. If you don't and you lose your ticket, anyone can cash it in and you can't prove it was yours.

CHAPTER NINE

LOSING TICKETS

I know that those of you who are reading this book are not stupid. You know that not all the tickets you buy are going to be winners. In fact, most of your tickets are going to be losing tickets. Everyone has losing tickets, I have losing tickets. But did you know that those losing tickets are valuable? What do most people do with their losing tickets? That's right, they throw them away. Well, don't. Put them in a box.

Whenever you win a large enough prize that the local merchant can't pay you on the spot, you must take your tickets to the lottery office to cash them in. If that amount is high enough (in Florida it is $5,000), the lottery office will deduct taxes from it. That's right, Uncle Sam must get paid. They will give you a tax form for you to include with your tax return for that year.

Now, here is where the losing tickets become important. If you win enough money during that year, you will be able to deduct the cost of those losing tickets, against the taxes that you would have to pay on those winnings. The amount of money you need to win to make this worthwhile and the amount of losing tickets you will be able to deduct will depend on various conditions. The best way to know exactly what you will be allowed to do is to check with your accountant. So put all of those losing tickets into a box.

I have a notepad on top of my box, and every time I add losing tickets to it, I write down the total amount of those tickets and add it to the total amount of losing tickets that are already in the box. This way I keep a running total throughout the year.

Be sure to do this; otherwise, if during the year you win enough to use those losing tickets in regard to your taxes, you're going to have to add up all those losing tickets at once come tax time.

CLOSING COMMENTS

So there you have it; these are the methods I use to play lottery games. These are the methods that have enabled me to win several lottery game grand prizes. **I can't promise or guarantee that you will win anything, but I hope you do.**

And remember, *don't spend more than you can afford.*

Here's to your first big win!

CREDITS

Richard Lustig	Creator & Author
Cosetta Lustig	Communications
Linda Ganzini (www.lindaganzini.com)	Book Design
Donald Lustig	Seminars
Jonathan Lustig	Marketing & Promotions

and finally...

Nicholas Lustig	Spending

AuthorHouse™
1663 Liberty Drive
Bloomington, IN 47403
www.authorhouse.com
Phone: 1-800-839-8640

First published by AuthorHouse 9/27/2010

ISBN: 978-1-4520-7746-8 (sc)

Printed in the United States of America

This book is printed on acid-free paper.

authorHOUSE®